ADELE

3RD EDITION

FOR PIANO SOLO

2 ALL I ASK

6 CHASING PAVEMENTS

9 EASY ON ME

12 HELLO

14 HOLD ON

22 HOMETOWN GLORY

19 LOVESONG

24 MAKE YOU FEEL MY LOVE

27 ROLLING IN THE DEEP

30 SKYFALL

34 SOMEONE LIKE YOU

39 TO BE LOVED

42 TURNING TABLES

46 WHEN WE WERE YOUNG

Cover photo by Gareth Cattermole/Getty Images for Adele

ISBN 978-1-70517-199-8

World headquarters, contact:
Hal Leonard
7777 West Bluemound Road
Milwaukee, WI 53213
Email: info@halleonard.com

In Europe, contact:
Hal Leonard Europe Limited
1 Red Place
London, W1K 6PL
Email: info@halleonardeurope.com

In Australia, contact:
Hal Leonard Australia Pty. Ltd.
4 Lentara Court
Cheltenham, Victoria, 3192 Australia
Email: info@halleonard.com.au

ALL I ASK

Words and Music by ADELE ADKINS,
BRUNO MARS, CHRIS BROWN
and PHILIP LAWRENCE

Moderately fast

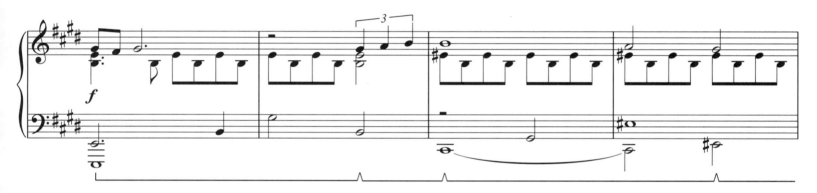

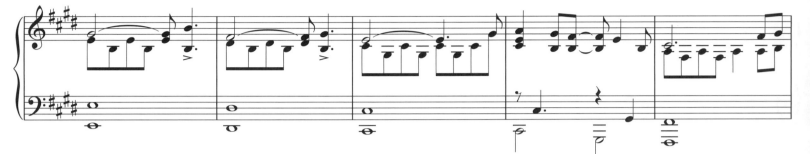

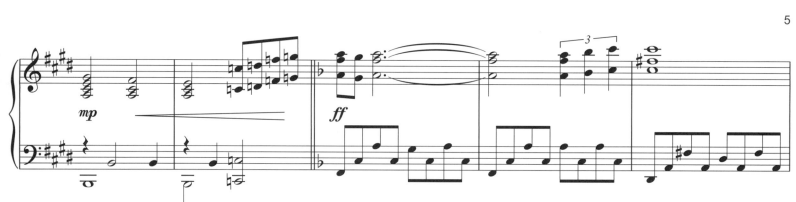

CHASING PAVEMENTS

Words and Music by ADELE ADKINS
and FRANCIS EG WHITE

CODA

EASY ON ME

Words and Music by ADELE ADKINS
and GREG KURSTIN

HELLO

Words and Music by ADELE ADKINS
and GREG KURSTIN

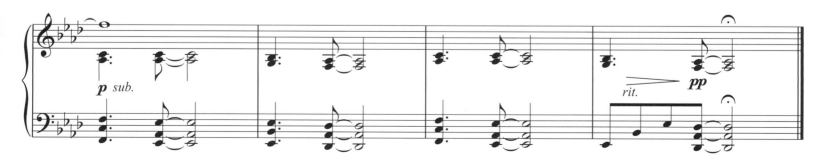

HOLD ON

Words and Music by ADELE ADKINS
and DEAN JOSIAH COVER

Medium Gospel

16

LOVESONG

Words and Music by ROBERT SMITH,
LAURENCE TOLHURST, SIMON GALLUP,
PAUL S. THOMPSON, BORIS WILLIAMS
and ROGER O'DONNELL

Easy groove

(acoustic guitar)

D.S. al Coda

CODA

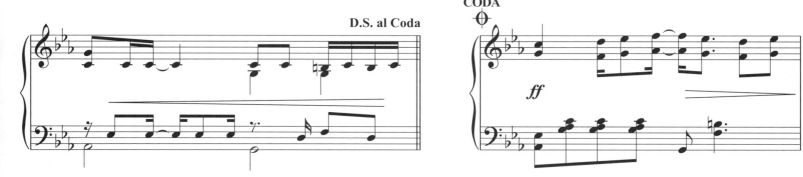

HOMETOWN GLORY

Words and Music by
ADELE ADKINS

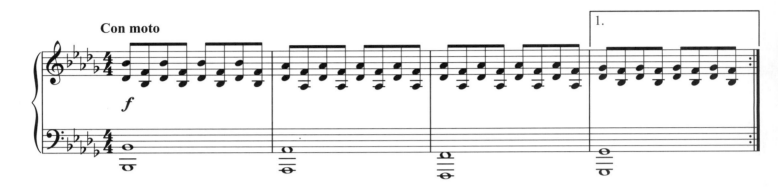

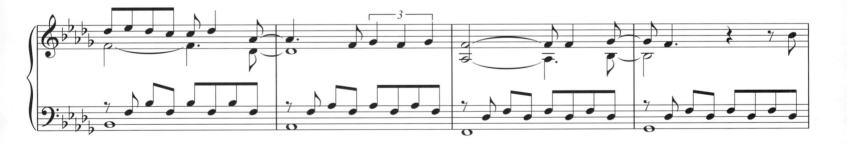

MAKE YOU FEEL MY LOVE

Words and Music by
BOB DYLAN

With a Gospel feel

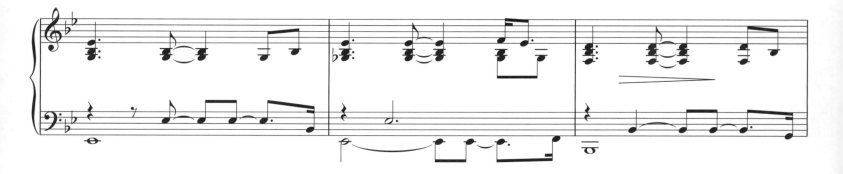

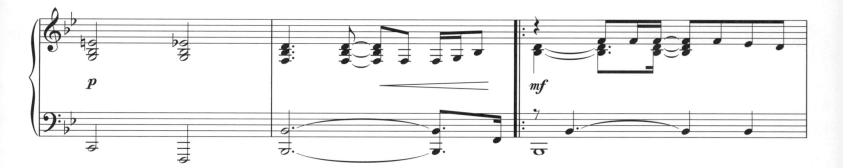

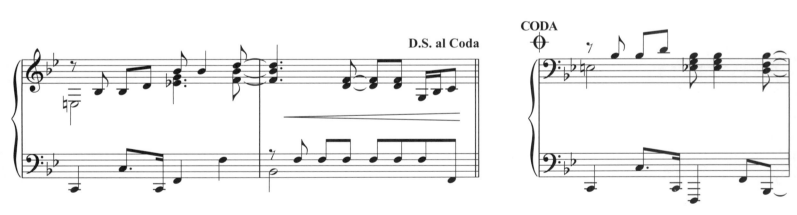

ROLLING IN THE DEEP

Words and Music by ADELE ADKINS
and PAUL EPWORTH

Soul groove

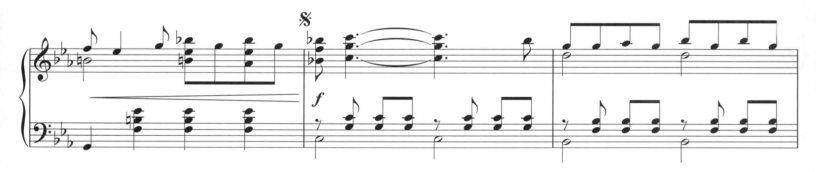

SKYFALL
from the Motion Picture SKYFALL

Words and Music by ADELE ADKINS
and PAUL EPWORTH

Moderately slow, mysterious

With pedal

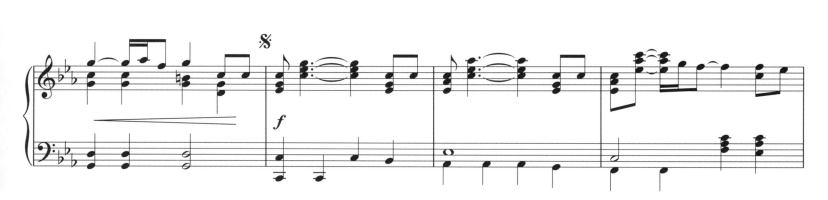

D.S. al Coda

CODA

SOMEONE LIKE YOU

Words and Music by ADELE ADKINS
and DAN WILSON

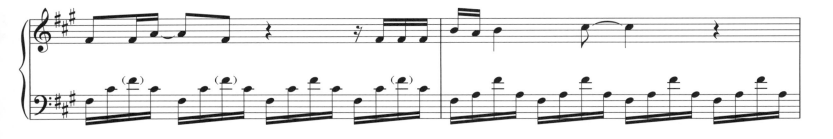

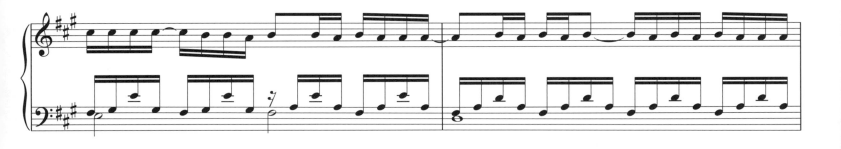

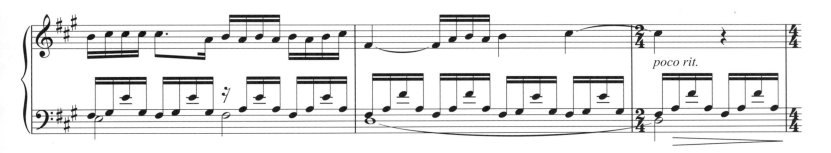

To Coda

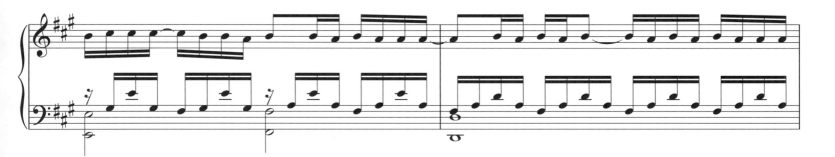

D.S. al Coda

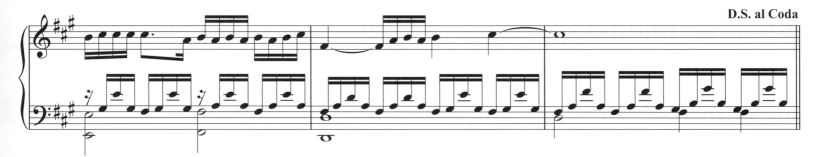

CODA

48

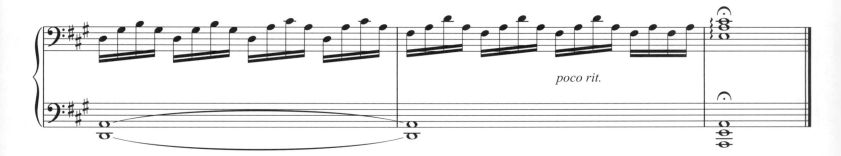

TO BE LOVED

Words and Music by ADELE ADKINS
and TOBIAS JESSO JR.

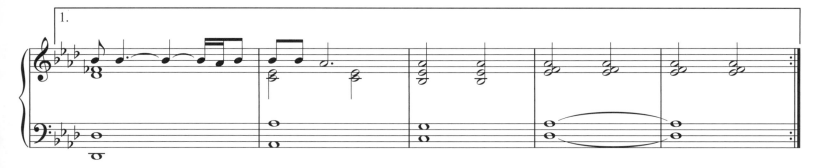

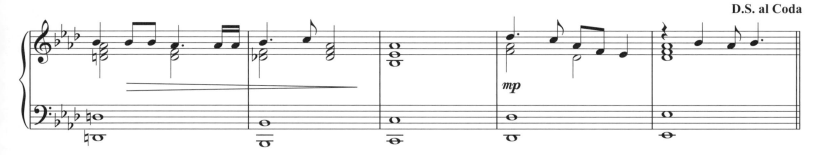

TURNING TABLES

Words and Music by ADELE ADKINS
and RYAN TEDDER

Moderate Ballad

With pedal

To Coda ⊕

WHEN WE WERE YOUNG

Words and Music by ADELE ADKINS
and TOBIAS JESSO JR.

Slowly, tenderly

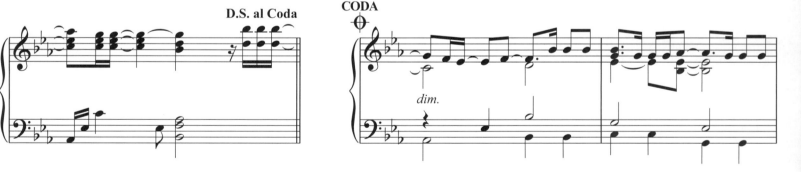